God Hides His Secrets

Words by P. J. Peregrine

Illustrations by Rhonda Robertson

© 2020 P.J. Peregrine
pjperegrine@gmail.com

All rights reserved. No part of this book may be reproduced in any form or by any means without prior written permission from the author.

Layout design by Rhonda Robertson

ISBN-13:978-1729777466
ISBN-10:1729777465

for Nayomie Rayne Gottlieb "Flower"

God hides His secrets under the sea.

He talks to seashells, and they talk to me.

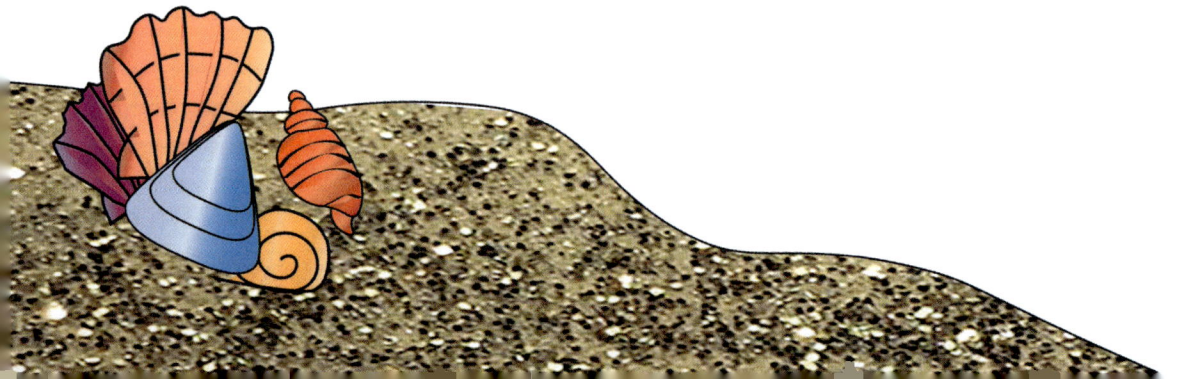

God hides His secrets up in the tree.

He whispers to birdies, and they sing to me.

God hides His secrets up in the skies.

His stars tell His stories and answer my "why's."

God hides His secrets in whiskers and fur.
I hear His wisdom in Kitty's soft purr.

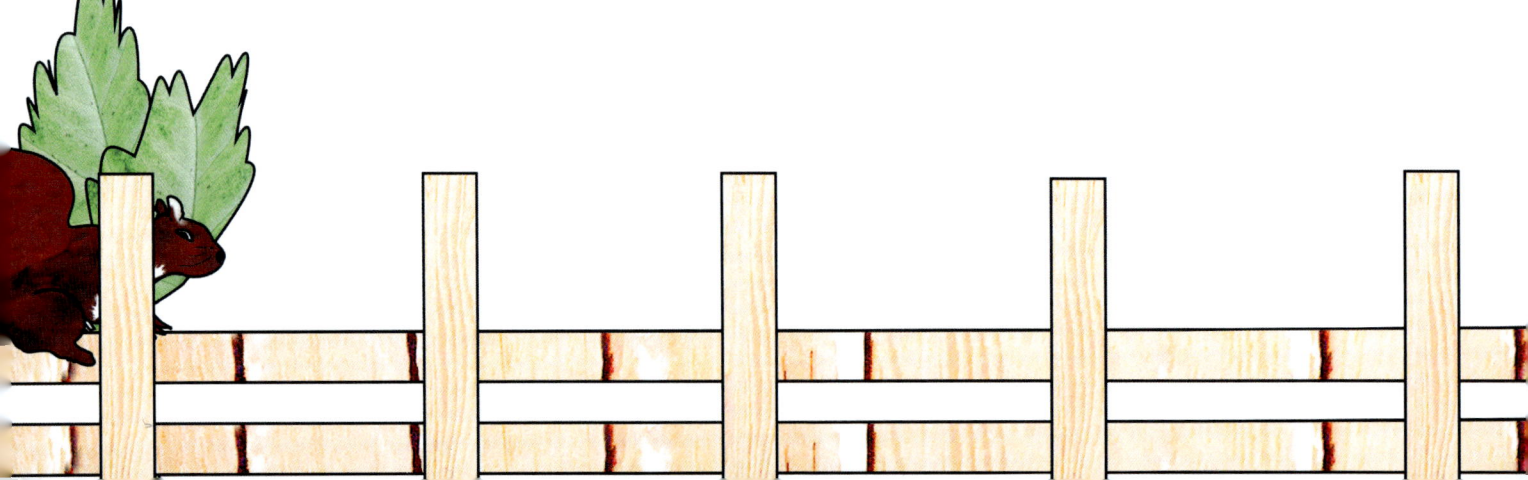

God hides His secrets under the earth.
He tucks seeds in bed, and they sprout up new birth.

God hides His secrets in rivers and streams.
They gurgle His thoughts and carry His dreams.

God hides His secrets in petals and stems.
His majesty calls me through glistening gems.

God hides His secrets in lightning and thunder.
He sprinkles down snowflakes that fill me with wonder.

God hides His secrets in rocks, leaves and wings.
Big words are spoken by very small things.

God hides His secrets in every design
for me to seek and for me to find.

His majesty calls me…

Ways you can use this book:

1. Go on an outing with your child to your back yard, a park or forest. Explore the rocks, leaves and acorns you find. What can your child learn from these things? What might God be speaking to your child through His great works?

2. Take your time reading and discussing each Scripture in the next section with your child.

3. Have your child draw pictures to depict some of the Scriptures or any of the topics in this book. Smaller children could make paper cutouts of stars, snowflakes, birds, seashells, animals or plants.

4. Look up some science ideas that confirm things in the book:

- Why do seashells sound like the sea when we put them to our ears?

- What are birds singing? Why do they sing in the morning? Did you know that the sun sings, too?

- The constellations, it has been discovered, tell the story of the Gospel.

5. Every snowflake is different, just like every fingerprint. Find enlarged pictures of snowflakes and marvel with your child over their beautiful design.

6. Turn an apple on its side and slice it to see the flower-like design inside.

7. Plant a bean and discuss how it had to stop being a bean to become a plant. You can extend the metaphor by discussing how Jesus' death resulted in life for us all.

…and fills me with wonder.

Scripture References

Secrets Under the Sea

God said to Job:

"Who closed the flood gates
as the sea gushed from the womb?
Who covered it with clouds
and wrapped it in darkness?
I set the limits for the sea
and put it behind locked gates.
I said to the sea, 'You can come this far, but no farther.
This is where your proud waves will stop.'
                    Job 38:8-11

Secrets Up in the Tree

The birds of the sky nest by the waters; they sing among the branches.
                    Psalm 104:12

Secrets Up in the Skies

The heavens proclaim the glory of God.
The skies display his craftsmanship.
Day after day they continue to speak; night after night they make him known.
They speak without a sound or word; their voice is never heard.
Yet their message has gone throughout the earth, and their words to all the world.
God has made a home in the heavens for the sun.
It bursts forth like a radiant bridegroom after his wedding.
It rejoices like a great athlete eager to run the race.
                    Psalm 19:1-5

Secrets in Whiskers and Fur

How many are your works, Lord!
In wisdom you made them all; the earth is full of your creatures.
                    Psalm 104:24

Scripture References

Secrets Under the Earth

Then God said,

"I give you every seed-bearing plant on the face of the whole earth and every tree that has fruit with seed in it. They will be yours for food."
Genesis 1:29

Very truly I tell you, unless a kernel of wheat falls to the ground and dies, it remains only a single seed. But if it dies, it produces many seeds.
John 12:24

Secrets in Rivers and Streams

He turned the desert into pools of water and the parched ground into flowing springs.
Psalm 107:35

He makes springs pour water into the ravines; it flows between the mountains. They give water to all the beasts of the field; the wild donkeys quench their thirst.
Psalm 104:10-11

Secrets in Glistening Gems

At once I was in the Spirit, and there before me was a throne in heaven with someone sitting on it. And the one who sat there had the appearance of jasper and ruby. A rainbow that shone like an emerald encircled the throne. Surrounding the throne were twenty-four other thrones, and seated on them were twenty-four elders. They were dressed in white and had crowns of gold on their heads... They lay their crowns before the throne and say:

"You are worthy, our Lord and God, to receive glory and honor and power, for you created all things, and by your will they were created and have their being."
Revelatiion 4:2-4, 10-11

Secrets in Lightning, Thunder, and Snow

"Have you entered the storehouses of the snow, or have you seen the storehouses of the hail?"
Job 38:22

Scripture References

Secrets in Small Things

There are four things on earth that are small but unusually wise:

Ants—they aren't strong, but they store up food all summer.
Hyraxes [rock badgers]—they aren't powerful, but they make their homes among the rocks.
Locusts—they have no king, but they march in formation.
Lizards—they are easy to catch, but they are found even in kings' palaces.

Proverbs 30:24-28

Secrets in Every Design

It is the glory of God to conceal things, but the glory of kings is to search things out.

Proverbs 25:2

Praise the Lord, everything He has created,
everything in all His kingdom.
Let all that I am praise the Lord.
Psalm 103:22

Other Books by P.J. Peregrine

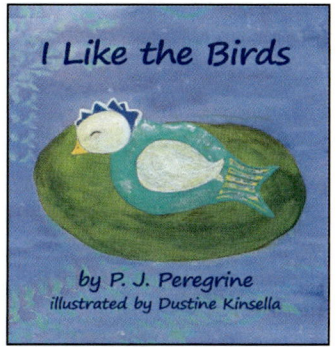
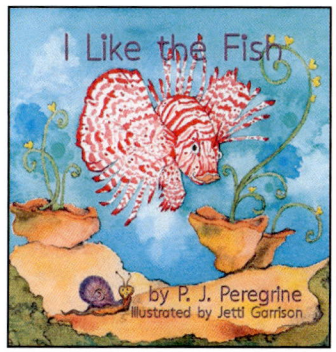

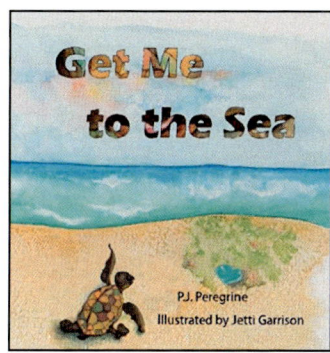
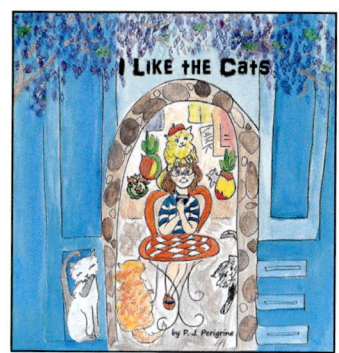

Made in the USA
Monee, IL
06 September 2021